# Honey Girl

## The Hawaiian Monk Seal

by Jeanne Walker Harvey
illustrated by Shennen Bersani

In Hawai'i, anyone who spots a Hawaiian monk seal feels lucky. These marine mammals are endangered and most live far away, by islands without people.

But one Hawaiian monk seal named Honey Girl is often seen around the North Shore of Oahu. Honey Girl is a local favorite. She's called "Super Mom" because by the age of fifteen she had raised seven pups.

Yet soon after Honey Girl weaned her seventh pup, she ran into trouble.

It was a warm November day when kite surfers reported seeing a monk seal covered in green algae. It was floating in the ocean. Why wasn't it moving?

Marine mammal experts arrived, but the monk seal was gone. Perhaps it had been caught in fishing line, and then freed itself. A search began and the animal was found. The tag on its back flipper was marked "R5AY." It was Honey Girl!

But the scientists couldn't help her until she came out of the water.

Honey Girl finally dragged herself onto the beach. Terribly thin, she lay limp on the sand. An ulua fishhook was caught in her cheek. Her tongue was cut by a fishing line and had gotten infected. She hadn't been able to catch or swallow food for several weeks. Unable to eat, she would soon starve. Could she be saved?

The scientists surrounded her. Honey Girl raised her head as if to bark, but she couldn't make a sound. The people gently lifted her into a crate in the back of a truck. They drove her across the island to Waikiki Aquarium.

The first step was to remove the fishhook from Honey Girl's cheek. For two days, she received round-the-clock care.

But Honey Girl needed even more help. Her tongue had been injured from the fishing line wrapped around it. Again, she was loaded into a crate.

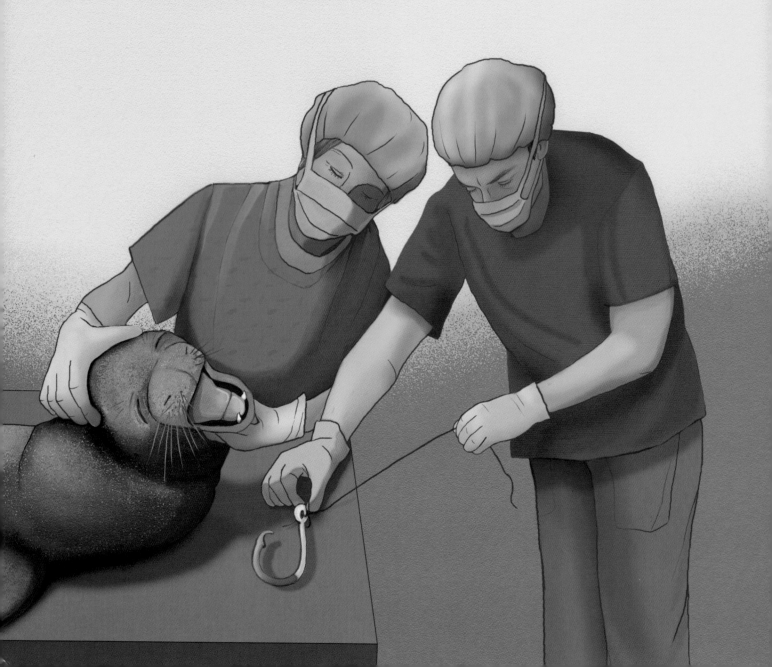

At the Honolulu Zoo, veterinarians performed the first known operation on the tongue of a Hawaiian monk seal. They were pleased that half of her tongue was saved.

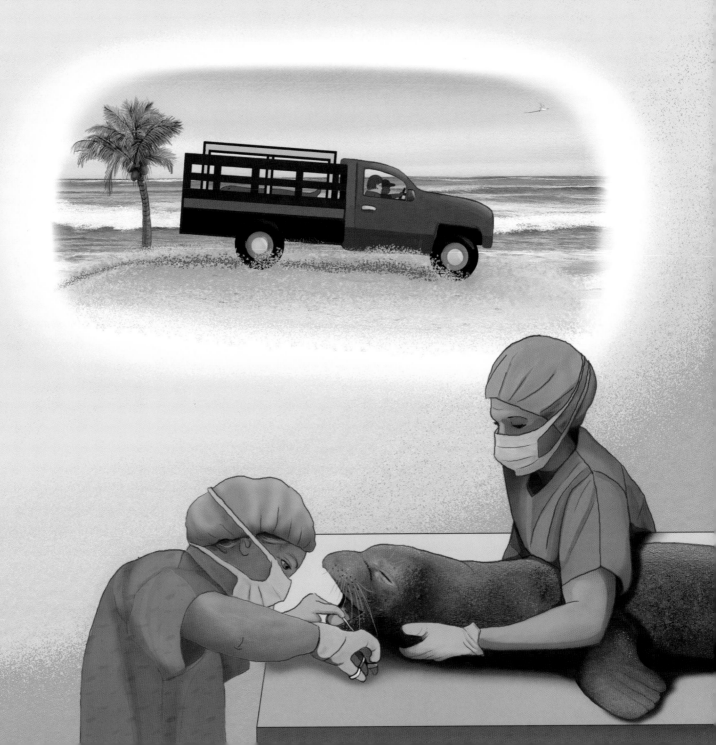

At first, she couldn't swallow her usual food of fish, squid, octopus, eels, crabs, shrimp or lobsters. So Honey Girl was fed a "seal shake" of ground-up herring and water through a tube.

But on her own, Honey Girl wouldn't eat small, frozen herring tossed into her pool. The scientists were worried she wouldn't be able to eat fish. If she couldn't eat fish, she couldn't return to the ocean.

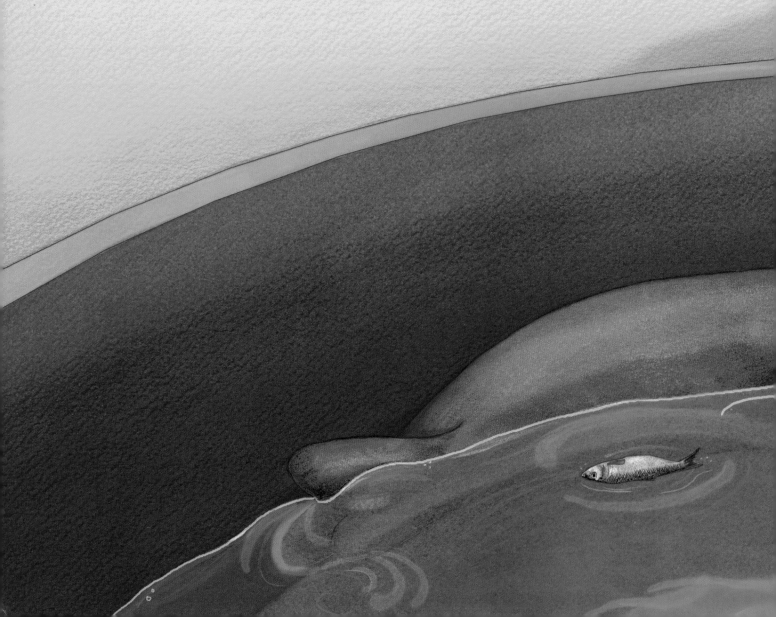

On Thanksgiving Day, Honey Girl caught and ate live tilapia. Honey Girl was perking up!

Thirteen days after her rescue, the scientists decided she could go home.

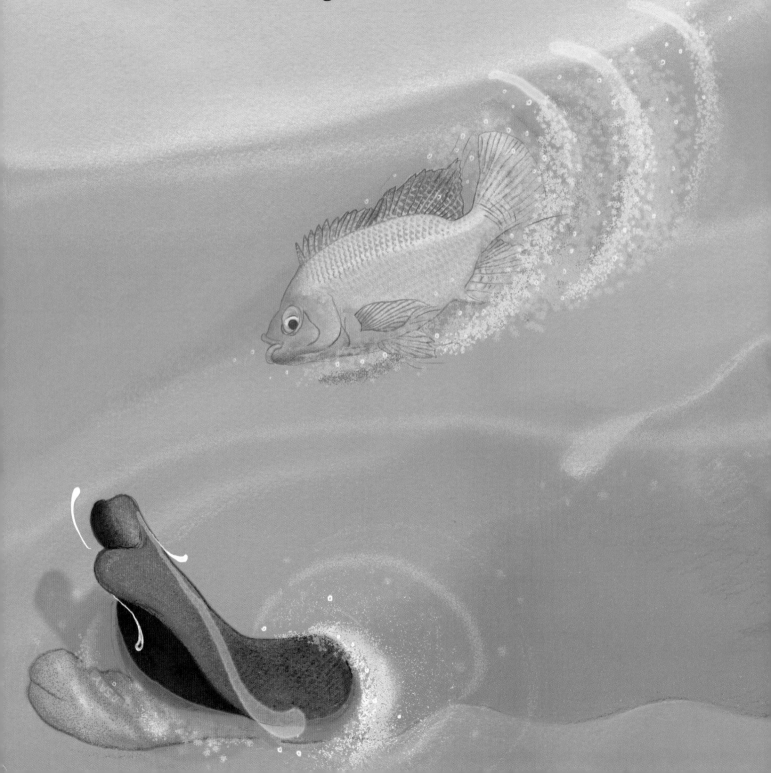

In the early morning sunshine, well-wishers gathered to welcome Honey Girl to Turtle Bay, just north of where she had been found on Sunset Beach. She hadn't regained any weight, but she was much improved.

Everyone quietly watched as Honey Girl scooted out of the crate and across the sand. She rested on the shore next to the foamy water. Finally, she dove into the waves. Honey Girl was like a "dog running in the rough seas," which is the meaning of the Hawaiian name for monk seals: *'īlioholoikauaua* (ilio-holo-i-ka-ua-ua).

Over the next month, a tracking device attached to Honey Girl's back showed where she swam. The scientists were pleased to learn that she traveled far from shore and back again. She was hunting for food.

Many times, she was seen resting on the beaches. And fortunately, she didn't suffer any more run-ins with fishing gear.

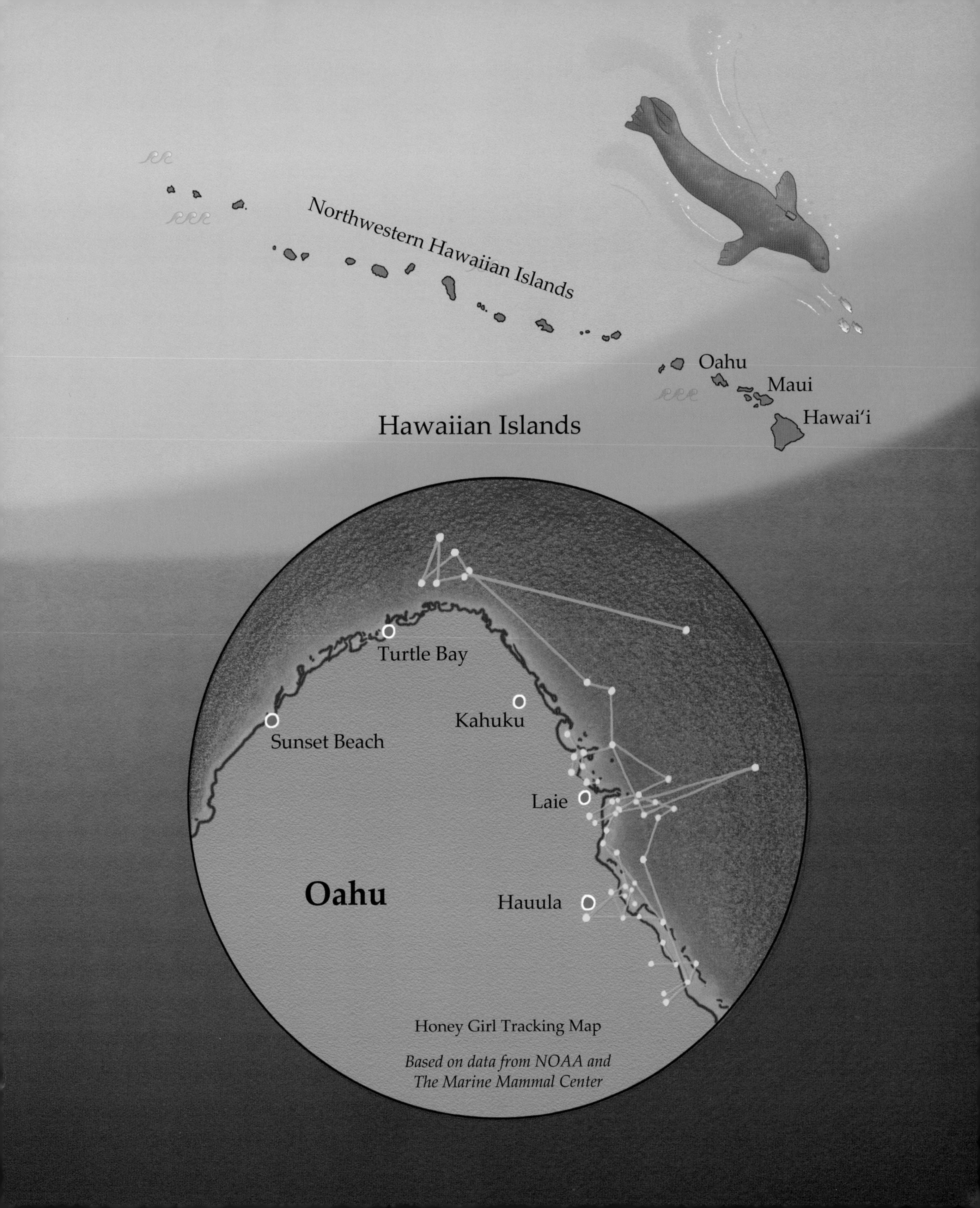

Northwestern Hawaiian Islands

Hawaiian Islands

Oahu
Maui
Hawai'i

Turtle Bay

Kahuku

Sunset Beach

Laie

Hauula

**Oahu**

Honey Girl Tracking Map

*Based on data from NOAA and
The Marine Mammal Center*

Scientists still wondered if she was gaining enough weight. A few weeks after she had been released, they caught her again. She was examined. They were relieved to see she was indeed heavier. And her tongue was healing without an infection.

Honey Girl grew rounder and her coat sleek and silver.

And then the best news of all: Honey Girl was pregnant! No one had been sure if she could eat enough for herself and a pup after being injured so seriously.

But she did! The islanders celebrated Honey Girl's birth of Meli, the first Hawaiian monk seal pup of the New Year. And as if to welcome their new sister, two of Honey Girl's other daughters, La'akea and Kaikaina, joined Meli and their mother on the Turtle Bay beach.

For about six weeks, Honey Girl, just like all Hawaiian monk seal mothers, stayed on the beach with Meli and protected her. Meli nuzzled up to her mother, and Honey Girl snuggled Meli as they rolled in the sand.

Day and night, volunteers prevented curious onlookers and their dogs from getting too close. If frightened, Honey Girl might have hurt someone while trying to protect her pup.

Without returning to the sea for food while nursing Meli, Honey Girl lost about half of her body weight. Honey Girl weaned her. It was time for Meli to learn to hunt for herself.

Now Honey Girl could return to the ocean to feed. The thin, exhausted Honey Girl inched across the sand. She paused in the rough waves. Then she pushed herself into the water and gracefully swam away.

The very next year, Honey Girl gave birth to yet another pup. And later that same year, Honey Girl became a grandmother for the first known time. Her daughter, Ua Malie, had a pup named Holokai.

Hopefully, in the years to come, many more Hawaiian monk seals will be spotted off the islands of Hawai'i. Meanwhile, Honey Girl is helping her endangered species by giving birth to healthy pups that then can have more pups.

*Mahalo*, thank you, to Honey Girl, the "Super Mom" Hawaiian monk seal.

# For Creative Minds

## Hawaiian Monk Seal Life Cycle

Hawaiian monk seals give birth to one pup at a time, about once a year. Most Hawaiian monk seals are born in spring and summer, but they can be born at any time of year.

Newborns weigh 30-40 pounds (13-18 kg) and are about 3.3 feet (1 meter) long when they are born. They have black, short, fuzzy hair all over their bodies.

Pups stay with their mothers and nurse for about six weeks after birth. The mothers live on the beach and don't eat during this entire time.

When pups are six weeks old and weigh 150-200 pounds (68-90 kg), their mothers return to the ocean. The pups are left alone on the beach. They learn how to take care of themselves.

As the seals grow, their bodies change. The black fur molts (falls out) and grows back dark silver or grey. The fur on their bellies is lighter. Sometimes algae grow on their fur and turn them green, red, or brown.

Female monk seals are ready to mate when they are 5-9 years old. Hawaiian monk seals live for 25-30 years.

Hawaiian monk seals are 7-7.5 feet (2.1-2.3 meters) long and weigh 375-450 pounds (170-204 kg).

*Is an adult Hawaiian monk seal bigger or smaller than an adult human?*

# Fun Facts

## What makes a mammal?

- has a spine or spinal column
- breathes oxygen from the air
- is warm-blooded
- has hair or fur
- gives birth to live young (most)
- produces milk to feed young

Hawaiian monk seals are a type of marine mammal called a **pinniped**. Walruses; eared seals, such as sea lions and fur seals; and earless seals (true seals) are all different types of pinnipeds. Monk seals get their name from the loose skin around their necks. It looks like a monk's cowl.

Hawaiian monk seals live in the waters around the Hawaiian Islands in the Pacific Ocean. They are the state mammal of Hawai'i!

They spend most of their time in the ocean, hunting prey. But they do take breaks to bask in the sun on sandy beaches.

Most Hawaiian monk seals stay near the Northwestern Hawaiian Islands, but they have been spotted on all of the Main Hawaiian Islands as well. They return to the same areas every year. Only 10-15% of Hawaiian monk seals travel between islands.

Hawaiian monk seals are predators. They hunt fish, crabs (crustaceans), and octopus and squids (cephalopods). They eat 3-8% of their body weight every day. This means a Hawaiian monk seal that weighs 400 lb (181 kg) would eat 12-32 lb (5.4-14.5 kg) of food every day!

Generally, Hawaiian monk seals hunt for food just off the coast, in waters 60-300 feet deep (18-91 meters). But they can dive deeper than 1,000 feet (330 meters) in search of food.

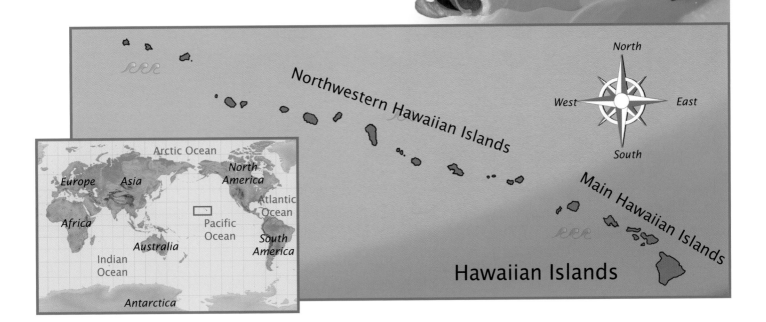

Northwestern Hawaiian Islands

North

West — East

South

Main Hawaiian Islands

Arctic Ocean

Europe Asia

North America

Atlantic Ocean

Africa

Pacific Ocean

South America

Australia

Indian Ocean

Antarctica

Hawaiian Islands

# Conservation

Hawaiian monk seals are **endangered**. If humans don't help them, Hawaiian monk seals could go extinct. In 2016, there were only 1,300 Hawaiian monk seals left in the world.

Why are Hawaiian monk seals endangered?

- Seals have to compete with sharks and other predators for food. Some young seals can't get enough to eat.
- Sharks hunt and eat young seals.
- Some humans hurt or kill seals.
- Adult male seals sometimes attack female seals or juveniles.
- Seals need low-lying beaches where they can give birth and nurse their pups. Many beaches are being lost to erosion, sea level rise, or human development.
- Fishing nets and hooks, like the one that injured Honey Girl, can harm or kill seals.
- Seals catch diseases from other seals, humans, or dogs.
- Seals get tangled in or injured by marine debris—lost fishing nets, plastic, and other human trash.
- Some humans try to swim or play with young seals. When wild animals get used to humans, they sometimes try to get too close to humans. This is dangerous for the animals, who can be injured or killed. It can also be dangerous for the humans. The seals may not seem scary when they are small, but the way they "play" in the water can be dangerous for humans.

But even though Hawaiian monk seals are in trouble, there is still hope.

Numerous federal and Hawaiian organizations are working together to conserve Hawaiian monk seals. When seals or other marine mammals are injured or stranded, teams of scientists go out to rescue the animals. They treat the animals' injuries and return them to the wild, just like they did with Honey Girl.

By tagging and tracking seals, scientists can learn more about their behavior in the wild, and how to help them.

Too many Hawaiian monk seals are injured or killed by humans, or get used to being around humans. Humans can learn about and stop harmful behaviors that hurt Hawaiian monk seals. When people act responsibly and stay a safe distance away from seals, humans and seals can share Hawai'i's beaches and shores in peace.

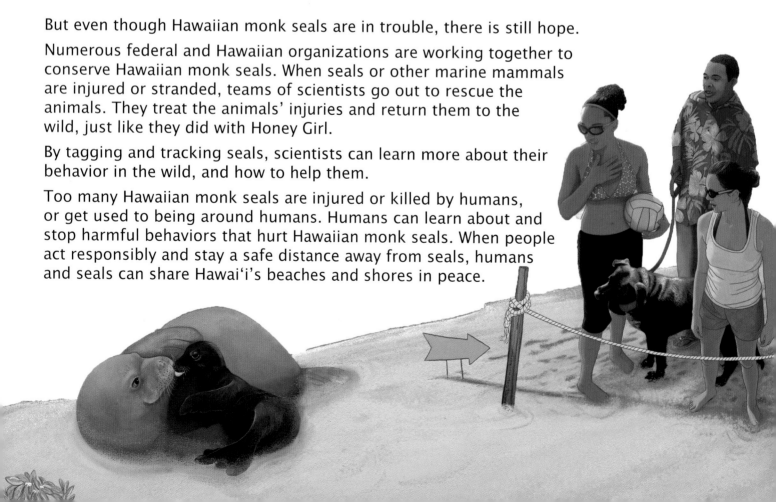

# Rescue and Rehabilitation

Sometimes even wild animals like Honey Girl need help. It takes a lot of people working together to rescue injured animals and rehabilitate them so they can go back to the wild.

Put the following steps of Honey Girl's journey in order to unscramble the words.

The scientists took Honey Girl to Waikiki Aquarium. There, veterinarians removed the fishhook.

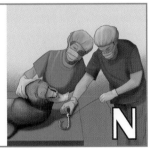

Finally, Honey Girl was well enough to eat on her own. She could go home to the ocean.

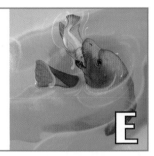

People on the beach saw that Honey Girl was in trouble. They called for help.

Marine mammal experts came to look for her. They waited for Honey Girl to come to the beach.

Scientists watched Honey Girl's movements through her tracking device. She was doing well.

After surgery, Honey Girl was still too weak to eat. Animal experts made special "seal shakes" for her to drink.

Honey Girl fully recovered from her adventure and went on to have more pups.

Honey Girl still needed more help. She went to the Honolulu Zoo for surgery on her tongue.

Answer: monk seal

I dedicate this book to my amazing sons, Will and Scott, who were with me when I first saw a Hawaiian monk seal (possibly Honey Girl!) at the Turtle Bay beach. Thank you to Dr. Michelle Barbieri, Hawaiian Monk Seal Health Program Coordinator for The Marine Mammal Center/Ke Kai Ola and NOAA Fisheries, who was with Honey Girl in her rescue, rehabilitation and release, and who generously shared her experiences and expertise with me. And I appreciate all the volunteers, veterinarians, scientists and staff at NOAA Fisheries Hawaiian Monk Seal Research Program (HMSRP), Pacific Islands Regional Office, Waikiki Aquarium, Honolulu Zoo, Hawaiian Monk Seal Response Team Oahu (HMSRTO), and The Marine Mammal Center who worked together to rescue and care for Honey Girl. My heartfelt thanks to those who helped me with this story: The Marine Mammal Center's Executive Director Dr. Jeff Boehm and Story and Communications Curator Sarah van Schagen, Lanikai General Store owner Donna Festa, the committed volunteers in Hawaii featured in the MonkSealMania blog, and my dear family and friends who always encourage me in my writing endeavors. And special thanks to my friend and talented illustrator, Shennen Bersani, and expert editor Katie Hall.—JWH

To research these illustrations, I flew from Boston to Oahu to visit the habitats of Honey Girl. I met with Monk Seal volunteers and workers who shared their stories of R5AY and Monk Seals. My heartfelt thanks goes out to Donna Festa (Lanikai General Store owner), Diane Gabriel (guide to Honey Girl's beach habitats), Dana Jones (helped Honey Girl during rehab), and D. B. Dunlap (The Seal Whisperer). I also visited Deb Wickham on the Big Island (Ke Kai Ola Hospital for Monk Seals at Kailua-Kona). A key highlight was visiting the Mt. Kilauea active volcano on the Big Island and climbing over lava formations to reach a beach and observe a seal at sunset. My ultimate heartfelt thanks goes to my friend and author Jeanne Walker Harvey. Aloha!—SB

Thanks to The Marine Mammal Center and to Dr. Michelle Barbieri, Wildlife Veterinary Medical Officer with NOAA's Hawaiian Monk Seal Research Program, for verifying the accuracy of the information in this book.

The author donates a portion of her royalties to The Marine Mammal Center's Ke Kai Ola hospital in Kona, Hawai'i, which is the first rehabilitation facility for Hawaiian Monk Seals.

Library of Congress Cataloging-in-Publication Data

Names: Harvey, Jeanne Walker, author. | Bersani, Shennen, illustrator.
Title: Honey girl : the Hawaiian monk seal / by Jeanne Walker Harvey ;
   illustrated by Shennen Bersani.
Description: Mount Pleasant, SC : Arbordale Publishing, [2017] | Audience:
   Ages 4-8. | Audience: K to grade 3. | Includes bibliographical references.
Identifiers: LCCN 2016043589 (print) | LCCN 2016045182 (ebook) | ISBN
   9781628559217 (english hardcover) | ISBN 9781628559224 (english pbk.) |
   ISBN 9781628559231 (spanish pbk.) | ISBN 9781628559248 (English
   Downloadable eBook) | ISBN 9781628559262 (English Interactive
   Dual-Language eBook) | ISBN 9781628559255 ( Spanish Downloadable eBook) |
   ISBN 9781628559279 (Spanish Interactive Dual-Language eBook)
Subjects: LCSH: Hawaiian monk seal--Juvenile literature. | Wildlife
   rescue--Hawaii--Juvenile literature. | Rare mammals--Juvenile literature.
   | Seals (Animals)--Juvenile literature.
Classification: LCC QL737.P64 H3745 2017 (print) | LCC QL737.P64 (ebook) |
   DDC 599.79/5--dc23
LC record available at https://lccn.loc.gov/2016043589

Translated into Spanish: Honey Girl: *La foca monje de Hawái*

Lexile® Level: AD 830

key phrases: based on a true story, basic needs, conservation, endangered species, Hawai'i, Hawaiian monk seal, health, life cycle, map, rehabilitation, seal, sequence, wildlife rescue

Bibliography:
"Hawaiian Monk Seal (Neomonachus Schauinslandi)" NOAA Fisheries. n.d. Web. 13 Sept. 2016.
"Hawaiian Monk Seal." The Marine Mammal Center. N.p., n.d. Web. 13 Sept. 2016.
"Hawaiian Monk Seal Research Program." NOAA Fisheries, Pacific Islands Fisheries Science Center. n.d. Web. 13 Sept. 2016.
Kalman, Bobbie. **Endangered Monk Seals**. New York, NY: Crabtree Pub., 2004. Print.
Williams, Terrie M. *The Odyssey of KP2: An Orphan Seal, a Marine Biologist, and the Fight to save a Species*. New York: Penguin, 2012.
   Print.
Ziegler, Alan C. **Hawaiian Natural History, Ecology, and Evolution**. Honolulu: U of Hawai'i, 2002. Print.

Manufactured in China, December 2016
This product conforms to CPSIA 2008
First Printing

Arbordale Publishing
Mt. Pleasant, SC 29464
www.ArbordalePublishing.com